For C, B♭, E♭ & Bass Clef Instruments

1960s JAZZ

Play-Along

Trumpet: Jamie Breiwick
Alto and Tenor Sax: Eric Schoor
Piano: Mark Davis
Bass: Jeff Hamann
Drums: David Bayles
Recorded by Ric Probst at Tanner-Monagle Studio

To access online content, visit:
www.halleonard.com/mylibrary

Enter Code
1635-8761-4226-8235

ISBN 978-1-5400-2638-5

For more information on the Real Book series, including community forums, please visit
www.OfficialRealBook.com

Visit Hal Leonard Online at
www.halleonard.com

Contact Us:
Hal Leonard
7777 West Bluemound Road
Milwaukee, WI 53213
Email: info@halleonard.com

In Europe contact:
Hal Leonard Europe Limited
42 Wigmore Street
Marylebone, London, W1U 2RN
Email: info@halleonardeurope.com

In Australia contact:
Hal Leonard Australia Pty. Ltd.
4 Lentara Court
Cheltenham, Victoria, 3192 Australia
Email: info@halleonard.com.au

Contents

4

Ceora

— Lee Morgan

C VERSION

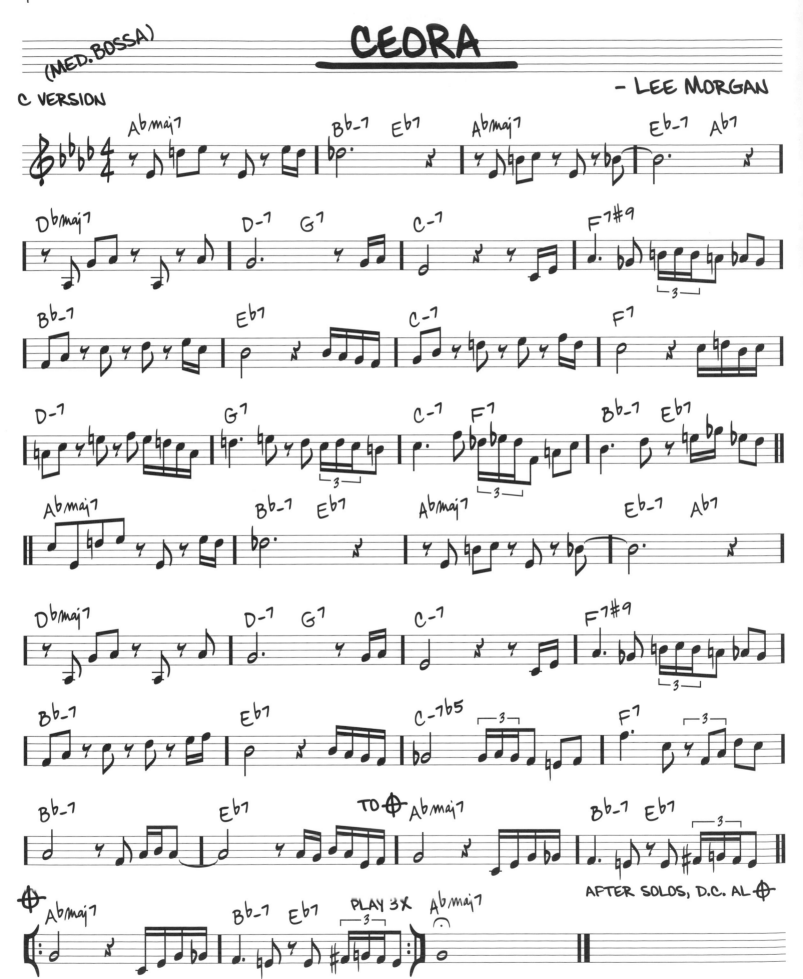

DAT DERE

— BOBBY TIMMONS

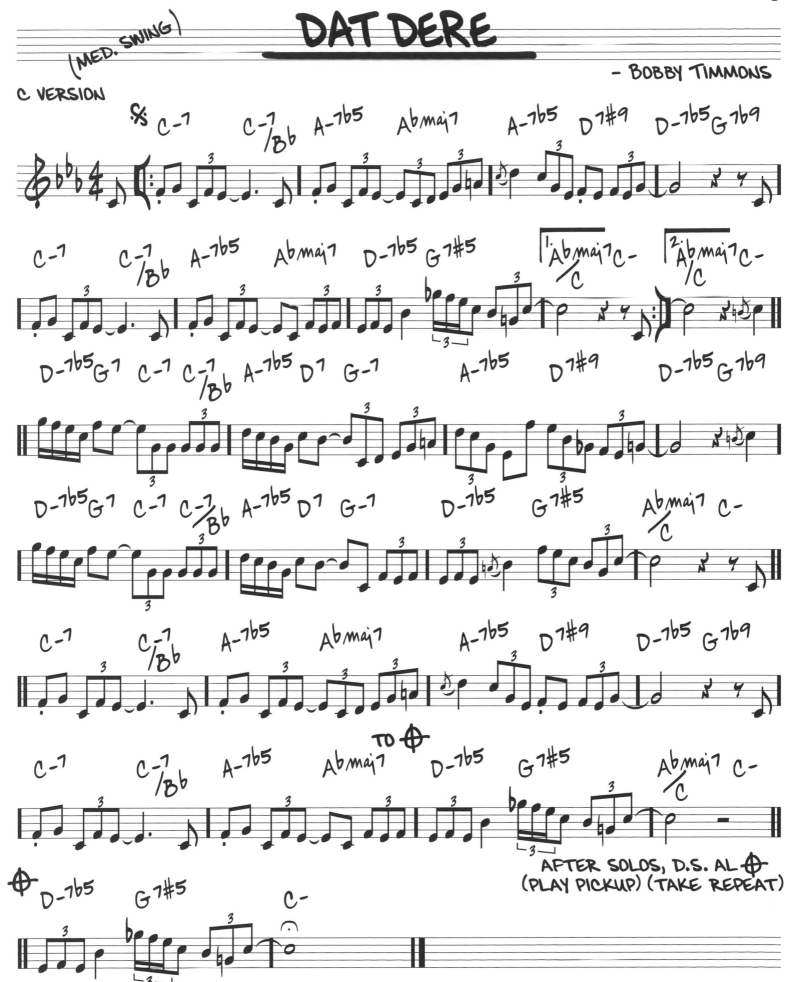

EQUINOX

Jeannine

– Duke Pearson

C VERSION

Recorda Me

(FAST BOSSA)

C VERSION

— JOE HENDERSON

FINE

AFTER SOLOS, D.S. AL FINE
(PLAY PICKUPS) (TAKE REPEAT)

STOLEN MOMENTS

— OLIVER NELSON

C VERSION

UP JUMPED SPRING

— FREDDIE HUBBARD

AFTER SOLOS, D.S. AL FINE
(PLAY PICKUPS) (TAKE REPEAT)

TOM THUMB

— Wayne Shorter

C VERSION

WINDOWS

C VERSION

— CHICK COREA

FINE
AFTER SOLOS, D.C. AL FINE

CEORA

— Lee Morgan

DAT DERE

— BOBBY TIMMONS

Dolphin Dance

— HERBIE HANCOCK

D.S. FOR SOLOS
AFTER SOLOS, D.S. AL ⊕

Equinox

Jeannine

— Duke Pearson

(UP)

Bb Version

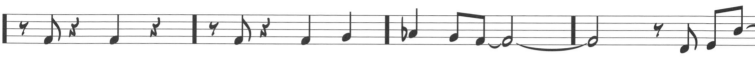

FINE

AFTER SOLOS, D.C. AL FINE
(TAKE REPEAT)

Recorda Me

— Joe Henderson

(FAST BOSSA)

Bb Version

FINE

AFTER SOLOS, D.S. AL FINE
(PLAY PICKUPS) (TAKE REPEAT)

Stolen Moments

TOM THUMB

– Wayne Shorter

WINDOWS

- CHICK COREA

CEORA

Eb Version

— Lee Morgan

(MED. BOSSA)

DAT DERE

— BOBBY TIMMONS

Dolphin Dance

Equinox

Jeannine

— Duke Pearson

Eb Version

(UP)

FINE

AFTER SOLOS, D.C. AL FINE
(TAKE REPEAT)

Recorda Me

— Joe Henderson

(FAST BOSSA)

Eb Version

FINE

AFTER SOLOS, D.S. AL FINE
(PLAY PICKUPS) (TAKE REPEAT)

Stolen Moments

Eb Version

— Oliver Nelson

UP JUMPED SPRING

– FREDDIE HUBBARD

Tom Thumb

— Wayne Shorter

Eb Version

WINDOWS

— CHICK COREA

Eb VERSION

FINE
AFTER SOLOS, D.C. AL FINE

CEORA

DAT DERE

— BOBBY TIMMONS

AFTER SOLOS, D.S. AL ⊕
(PLAY PICKUP) (TAKE REPEAT)

DOLPHIN DANCE

— HERBIE HANCOCK

D.S. FOR SOLOS
AFTER SOLOS, D.S. AL ⊕

Equinox

— JOHN COLTRANE

JEANNINE

– DUKE PEARSON

(UP)

𝄢: C VERSION

FINE

AFTER SOLOS, D.C. AL FINE
(TAKE REPEAT)

RECORDA ME

— JOE HENDERSON

(FAST BOSSA)

C VERSION

FINE

AFTER SOLOS, D.S. AL FINE
(PLAY PICKUPS) (TAKE REPEAT)

Stolen Moments

— Oliver Nelson

TOM THUMB

— WAYNE SHORTER

Windows

— CHICK COREA

FINE
AFTER SOLOS, D.C. AL FINE

THE REAL BOOK MULTI-TRACKS

TODAY'S BEST WAY TO PRACTICE JAZZ!
Accurate, easy-to-read lead sheets and professional, customizable audio tracks accessed online for 10 songs

1. MAIDEN VOYAGE PLAY-ALONG
Autumn Leaves • Blue Bossa • Doxy • Footprints • Maiden Voyage • Now's the Time • On Green Dolphin Street • Satin Doll • Summertime • Tune Up.
00196616 Book with Online Media...........$17.99

2. MILES DAVIS PLAY-ALONG
Blue in Green • Boplicity (Be Bop Lives) • Four • Freddie Freeloader • Milestones • Nardis • Seven Steps to Heaven • So What • Solar • Walkin'.
00196798 Book with Online Media $17.99

3. ALL BLUES PLAY-ALONG
All Blues • Back at the Chicken Shack • Billie's Bounce (Bill's Bounce) • Birk's Works • Blues by Five • C-Jam Blues • Mr. P.C. • One for Daddy-O • Reunion Blues • Turnaround.
00196692 Book with Online Media $17.99

4. CHARLIE PARKER PLAY-ALONG
Anthropology • Blues for Alice • Confirmation • Donna Lee • K.C. Blues • Moose the Mooche • My Little Suede Shoes • Ornithology • Scrapple from the Apple • Yardbird Suite.
00196799 Book with Online Media $17.99

5. JAZZ FUNK PLAY-ALONG
Alligator Bogaloo • The Chicken • Cissy Strut • Cold Duck Time • Comin' Home Baby • Mercy, Mercy, Mercy • Put It Where You Want It • Sidewinder • Tom Cat • Watermelon Man.
00196728 Book with Online Media $17.99

6. SONNY ROLLINS PLAY-ALONG
Airegin • Blue Seven • Doxy • Duke of Iron • Oleo • Pent up House • St. Thomas • Sonnymoon for Two • Strode Rode • Tenor Madness.
00218264 Book with Online Media $17.99

7. THELONIOUS MONK PLAY-ALONG
Bemsha Swing • Blue Monk • Bright Mississippi • Green Chimneys • Monk's Dream • Reflections • Rhythm-a-ning • 'Round Midnight • Straight No Chaser • Ugly Beauty.
00232768 Book with Online Media $17.99

8. BEBOP ERA PLAY-ALONG
Au Privave • Boneology • Bouncing with Bud • Dexterity • Groovin' High • Half Nelson • In Walked Bud • Lady Bird • Move • Witches Pit.
00196728 Book with Online Media $17.99

9. CHRISTMAS CLASSICS PLAY-ALONG
Blue Christmas • Christmas Time Is Here • Frosty the Snow Man • Have Yourself a Merry Little Christmas • I'll Be Home for Christmas • My Favorite Things • Santa Claus Is Comin' to Town • Silver Bells • White Christmas • Winter Wonderland.
00236808 Book with Online Media $17.99

10. CHRISTMAS SONGS PLAY-ALONG
Away in a Manger • The First Noel • Go, Tell It on the Mountain • Hark! the Herald Angels Sing • Jingle Bells • Joy to the World • O Come, All Ye Faithful • O Holy Night • Up on the Housetop • We Wish You a Merry Christmas.
00236809 Book with Online Media $17.99

11. JOHN COLTRANE PLAY-ALONG
Blue Train (Blue Trane) • Central Park West • Cousin Mary • Giant Steps • Impressions • Lazy Bird • Moment's Notice • My Favorite Things • Naima (Niema) • Syeeda's Song Flute.
00275624 Book with Online Media $17.99

12. 1950S JAZZ PLAY-ALONG
Con Alma • Django • Doodlin' • In Your Own Sweet Way • Jeru • Jordu • Killer Joe • Lullaby of Birdland • Night Train • Waltz for Debby.
00275647 Book with Online Media $17.99

13. 1960S JAZZ PLAY-ALONG
Ceora • Dat Dere • Dolphin Dance • Equinox • Jeannine • Recorda Me • Stolen Moments • Tom Thumb • Up Jumped Spring • Windows.
00275651 Book with Online Media $17.99

14. 1970S JAZZ PLAY-ALONG
Birdland • Bolivia • Chameleon • 500 Miles High • Lucky Southern • Phase Dance • Red Baron • Red Clay • Spain • Sugar.
00275652 Book with Online Media $17.99

15. CHRISTMAS TUNES PLAY-ALONG
The Christmas Song (Chestnuts Roasting on an Open Fire) • Do You Hear What I Hear • Feliz Navidad • Here Comes Santa Claus (Right down Santa Claus Lane) • A Holly Jolly Christmas • Let It Snow! Let It Snow! Let It Snow! • The Little Drummer Boy • The Most Wonderful Time of the Year • Rudolph the Red-Nosed Reindeer • Sleigh Ride.
00278073 Book with Online Media $17.99

HAL•LEONARD®
www.halleonard.com

Prices, content and availability subject to change without notice.